"Louis Gallo is an astute observer, who auspiciously employs poetry as a vehicle to portray the manifold nature of the world he is capable to grasp with all his senses, taking the readers along on his sensory ventures. In Clearing the Attic, this prolific and energetic poet again proves he excels in his honest and masterful approach to longer forms."

—Kristina Kočan,
Poet (Šara, 2008; Kolesa in murve, 2014; Šivje, 2018) Slovenia

"Louis Gallo's poems are always beautifully crafted yet accessible. They are savvy yet heartfelt, ironic but wistfully so."

—Gail Howard,
poetry editor, Thema Magazine

"A writer of fiction (much of it hilarious) and essays both scholarly and personal (often the product of deep study), as well as a teacher who has opened the minds of generations of students, Louis Gallo is a poet of many dimensions…"

—Ralph Adamo,
editor The Xavier Review, author of Ever

"…But reliant as he is on such colossi of often abstract, complex ideas, his poems first and foremost are always anchored with keen wit in the grit and gristle of a living world, one Gallo clearly finds both intoxicating and erotic…"

—Randall R. Freisinger,
author of Plato's Breath, winner of the May Swenson Poetry Prize, Utah State University Press

WHY IS THERE SOMETHING RATHER THAN NOTHING?

Why Is There Something Rather Than Nothing?

A collection of poems

by

LOUIS GALLO

Adelaide Books
New York / Lisbon
2021

WHY IS THERE SOMETHING RATHER THAN NOTHING?
A collection of poems
By Louis Gallo

Copyright © by Louis Gallo
Cover design © 2021 Adelaide Books

Published by Adelaide Books, New York / Lisbon
adelaidebooks.org

Editor-in-Chief
Stevan V. Nikolic

All rights reserved. No part of this book may be reproduced in any manner whatsoever without written permission from the author except in the case of brief quotations embodied in critical articles and reviews.

For any information, please address Adelaide Books
at info@adelaidebooks.org
or write to:
Adelaide Books
244 Fifth Ave. Suite D27
New York, NY, 10001

ISBN: 978-1-955196-16-1

Printed in the United States of America

for Cat, Claire & Madeleine, as usual

Contents

Acknowledgments **13**

I

    The Ten Most Important
    Questions of the Twentieth Century   *17*

II

    Westerns   *55*

    Milton, Santayana & Keats   *58*

    Amusement Park   *59*

    Archetypes   *61*

    Beethoven and Red Beans   *63*

    Break   *65*

    Dream of Cragsmoor   *66*

    Ergo Sum   *68*

    Faust   *70*

    Free Willy(y)   *71*

III

    Glass Booth   *75*

    Golem   *76*

    I Thought They Had Everything   *78*

    Ice Wagons   *80*

    Inspirations   *82*

    Traveling   *84*

    To or Not To   *86*

    Time as Disease   *87*

    Meem's House   *89*

    The Thing   *91*

    The Male Member   *93*

    You   *95*

    The Bearable Heaviness of Being   *96*

    The Wheel   *98*

    The Arrow of Time   *100*

    The Others   *102*

    Ornate Jewelry Boxes   *103*

    Song of a Man on the Verge   *104*

    Outer Space   *105*

IV

    Overheard   *109*

    Pelicans   *110*

    People   *112*

    Raccoon   *113*

WHY IS THERE SOMETHING RATHER THAN NOTHING?

Descartes Thrives **114**

Same Ole **116**

Some Punctuation Marks **118**

Natural Selection **120**

Superstition **123**

Access Denied **125**

Don't Forget to Dance **126**

Technology **128**

Thales **130**

The Book and Its Cover **132**

Surprised by Beauty in Brutality **134**

V

The Desire of Persistence **139**

When? **141**

Why Girls Should Not Eat Meat **143**

Old Age **145**

Old Library at Lee Circle **146**

Laundry **149**

Laocoön & Sons—Moving and Storage **152**

Distance Equals Rate X Time **154**

Listening to Scarlatti While Awaiting My Daughter to Cross the Drill Field **156**

A Special Case **158**

About the Author **161**

Acknowledgments

"The Ten Most Important Questions of the Twentieth Century," published as a chapbook of the same title, Prolific Pres; "Westerns," Floyd County Moonshine Literary Magazine; "Archetypes," "Some Punctuation Marks," "Ergo Sum," "Laocoon & Sons—Moving and Storage," Pennsylvania Literary Journal; "Pelicans," *Whurk Literary Journal*; "Time as Disease," "The Thing," "The Bearable Heaviness of Being," *Offcourse Literary Journal*; Arrow of Time," Adelaide Literary Magazine; "Access Denied," "Song of a Man on the Verge," *Contemporary American Voices*; "Meem's House," *Haunted Waters Press*

PART ONE

The Ten Most Important Questions of the Twentieth Century

musings in tongues

1

Why is there something rather than nothing?
             —Heidegger

Enchanted watery silence
cinched like silk ribbon
around the raw throat of hodgepodge
(mirage, chaos, noisy rag-a-muffin
tattooed with corpses and scorpions).
He sits in the Black Forest,
listens,
lives forever
and forgets he was a Nazi.
Ghostly Hindus
have touted the same
down the lotus instant
of millennia,
and still no one understands,
certainly not I
who use his fat doughy book
to flatten maple leaves.
Some bread
is too exquisitely sweet
for real tongues.

Louis Gallo

Ain't my problem, moans old blues man,
I got nuff wit di-verticula & glucomas.
Nothin' sumpin' now?
How come dis pile nothin'
in my han don't turn to hunrit dollez
& my fat old lady
wit her red bean & rice
& can o bacon grease
never disappear?
Nazi, dey put me in some gas too
I go close–
& I be nothin'.
You bet I howl
loud
like demon wit lizard skin.

to tally every crumb,
we favor accident
(though, mind you, who cares?).
Could be with a few
tumbles of such dice,
we'll wind up
sipping rum on the equator,
chastising the servants
and reciting *Esthetique du Mal*
to sandpipers.

WHY IS THERE SOMETHING RATHER THAN NOTHING?

2

What do women want?
            —Freud

We want his balls
ground into permanent silt.
This is so crucial we need not dwell
though something should be said
about the foul cigars and train rides
and those pale hysterical maidens
who, faint, confessed so little;
he took the dainty flushed
amaryllis in their cheeks
as arousal.
Quite a ruse, we grant—
to fondle inaccessible flesh
with your mind, against all odds.
And so desperate.

Well, I'd say we want men
to become women . . .
that's right,
so they know precisely
how we feel
and what we're thinking—
not necessarily why,
never why—

and can soothe
our every misery.
Of course, once they're women
we'll despise them and
hook with the Fabios
unloading crates of machinery
on oily wharves.
We'll change them too
when they can't get enough
of our soft ferocity.

Circe:
Oh, I'm still around.
Even back then we'd refined
the blunt saw-toothed approach,
shaved our legs, oiled our breasts
and learned where to dab
the lavender.
Check your latest *Cosmo*.
We don't dismember now,
chew up, turn them into pigs.
That creepy Orpheus
got too much mileage out of it.
And don't mention dream-boy
Hyacinthus who could still
melt my wax
even after his hacked
pieces scattered with the river.

WHY IS THERE SOMETHING RATHER THAN NOTHING?

Something to do with a war
between the sun and moon,
solar Apollo rising
from fecund, wet depths
to light up our skulls
with muscular neon.
Their broad strokes
smother you with overview.
I simply crave hard bone flesh
and make sure it craves me more,
because, honey, once spent,
they'll leave us panting
on a street corner
with nothing but a few tampons
in our hands.

3

Who's on first?
    –Abbot & Costello

When I was a kid whose voice
hadn't yet hardened
into the density of coal,
sure, I played ball in the street
with the gang.
I got picked last
because I struck out
every time or just about

Louis Gallo

and I couldn't catch a fly
if you threatened crucifixion.
But one magical time I did manage
a punt—is that what you call
those stupid baby hits?—and
slid onto first like butter
only because the baseman,
Tommy Cuccia (dead at forty),
started to retch and missed the play.
And that same day
I followed the parabola
of our dusty ball
with frayed red stitching
until it roosted precisely
in my glove.
I knew I'd clutched god
even if most of the sad, dreary season
I sulked in a field, terrified
that action might seek me out.
Who's on first?
I was once, only once,
by accident.
Holiness aside,
it's nothing to cherish.
Piss on first.

Dem last be first, bro,
when dey dead.

WHY IS THERE SOMETHING RATHER THAN NOTHING?

How come?
Dead, I mean.
Like brown leafs
roun Halloween.
Ax me,
brown leaf still
look last.

Godel's Theorem:
every closed system
leaks secretly into
a still greater closed system,
which leaks into another
ad infinitum.
St. Thomas said the same
of God, except God
requires neither equation
nor leak.
This suggests
that you are not you,
nor we ourselves;
that big fish
shrink in a larger bowl;
that something stupendous
is going on
right in our own back yards
where we store
the fertilizer.

4

Is the universe friendly?
                —Einstein

They peeled off his clothes
and shaved the skin
smooth as albumen—
pulled veins out like spaghetti,
shredded muscle and sinew,
sucked out the internal organs
(including the brain)
with puree machines.
They pulverized his bones
into fine acrid powder
that wafted all over town
with the first seasonal gusts.
Oh, they kept him alive,
as prescribed by law,
and it's reported
he still enjoys *Wheel of Fortune,*
the Weather Channel
and, most of all,
that sexy anchor-woman
whose swollen, bee-stung lips
pout headlines on MSNBC.
Without the equipment,
at fifty grand a day,
he wouldn't last a minute.
He can no longer speak

WHY IS THERE SOMETHING RATHER THAN NOTHING?

but we've learned
to translate nuances
in the aura shrouding
his phantom neurons.
I can touch the Edge from here,
he whispers, it's vast,
the boundary itself.
This side, the other,
mere packaging,
the skin of death & life,
not the onion.

Shaman dives into the Under World
toward a glowing orange room
scooped out of molten, magnetic core.
Korneke, he says to the bearded gnome
kneading flour, my spirit lags.
Korneke brushes his hands on the apron
and draws a phial from one of his pockets.
Shaman drinks the green syrup inside
and begins to convulse in rapture.
He finally passes out
only to wake inside the oven,
baked again like one of the loaves.
Korneke pulls him out when browned
and cracks open the crust with a mallet.
Ah, Korneke sighs, smells so good!
It takes more than memory, my friend,

Louis Gallo

you must live what you know
from moment to moment
and forget you know it.
Who are you? Shaman mumbles,
drowsy, caked with loose flour and sweat.
Korneke cackles, as usual, and winks.
That is the wrong question, he says.
All questions are wrong by nature–
the mind's flirtation with itself.
Become the bread you eat.
Try yourself, I used just the right amount
of yeast, hmm, so airy, aromatic
and fresh . . . like one of those
virtual particles you read about,
here and not here at the same time,
though time isn't quite the word
for Now
nor here for Everywhere.
And you're right to think
what I say sounds like so much shit.
I'm just a dumb baker.
Words can't touch
even one infinity
in a simple lump of dough.

Boltzmann gazed at
his own spidery figures

WHY IS THERE SOMETHING RATHER THAN NOTHING?

and promptly hanged himself.
Yet:
there's a hot little cactus
with sumptuous red blossoms
right outside The Desert Bar & Grill
in New Mexico.
Statistically, it grows backwards,
doesn't count in the overall diminution,
flaunts its beauty only to eyes
unaccustomed to the grotesque drift.
Comes down to calories and vectors,
the dispersal of heat
in each whirring atom.
That cactus shouldn't exist!
What nerve to defy the Law.
God knows we're trying to undo
the figures, however absolute,
but no chance Boltzmann
will ever unhang himself
or your bones reassemble
or that cactus bloom again
in the great cold stiffness to come.
Then again, once the earth was flat,
space, sodden with ether,
the stars, fixed sequins on a slate board.
Ash heaps of error.
Smell this flower.
Unknow thyself
and all the rest of it.

5

Where were you on the day
JFK was shot?
             —bunch of maudlin geezers

Nodding off in a physics class
at Tulane University.
Pulleys, fulcrums, leverage, mechanical advantage . . .
enough to finish you off long before
your own mechanical disadvantage
drives you to the edge of a wedge.
The professor, summoned from class,
returned pale-faced, shaken, undone.
Gentleman, he said, the president is dead.
Class dismissed.
I drove home in a torrential rain,
my eyes flooded as well,
heart resounding in its vat
with thumps of catastrophe.
JFK, the kind of guy your dad
would never be. Or you.
Now we know he was just another bum.
William Henry Harrison, my favorite,
never made it to the White House.
Or Harding, so trivial
he faded away like a soft pink stone.
Yet on that day
something fierce tore at me,
scattered my brains all over the car.

WHY IS THERE SOMETHING RATHER THAN NOTHING?

Old blues man:
I be pass out,
my haid hangin' low
in a long urinal.
Who dis Kan-dy?
A prez-i-dint?
Been so many prez-i-dent
& only one o me.
I got kilt once too.
When you say he die?
Hail, I done ready
went broke,
had firse chile
& got shot in my ass
by a woman so mean
she melt trombone
by lookin'.
Kan-dy, him soun like a baby.

Say your life
is a band of elastic
stretching
in only one direction
until there's no more give.
What about that other smooth via?
Why not stretch the other way?
Just a little magic
(not much to ask)

to sustain the illusion,
keep you bleating,
dodge the lead.

6

Do we run because we are afraid
or are we afraid because we run?
                –paraphrased loosely from William James

They jog through parks
and malls, up hills, across streams,
along railroad tracks dizzy with creosote.
They jog through plate glass,
into slaughterhouses and forest fires,
beyond mileposts and mercury vapor.
They jog into each other, into bulldozers,
tanks, gas pumps, boxcars, the Great Wall of China.
They jog to Jupiter, to Planet X, toward comets
and neutron stars, to the place where light stops.
They jog into molecules, down into nuclei
and electrons, neutrinos, and that pale finale,
the naked quark.
They jog drenched, on fire, frozen solid, sticky
with treacle, sprinkled with turmeric, basted,
pureed, minced, evaporated. They jog to Jesus
washing his hands in White's Truck Stop,
they jog to hell, they jog the chakras,
explode through the bleeding tantric skull.

WHY IS THERE SOMETHING RATHER THAN NOTHING?

They jog without arms or legs, blind, dumb,
palsied, rotting, blasted to bits, liquified.
They jog at prayer, at market, at toilets,
into the toilets and underground plumbing
of the metropolis, they jog in dreams,
in comas, in hallucinations and soap-like sanity.
They jog forever, backwards through time,
into the womb, out some other side of it,
that before-place, where they spin and float
and disappear, remembering nothing
beyond what has not yet happened
and what might.

Want to be cheerful?
Act cheerfully!
Thus Mr. James endowed
an entire tradition
of merriment, festoons,
confetti, after-dinner mints.
I think I can, I think I can, I think I can.
Chug chug–whoops, ran out of steam,
Casey, but I do believe I can.
WELL YOU'RE WRONG
rasps Cecil B. De Mille's
slithering green gas,
the Angel of Death.
Do we die because we live
or live because we die?

Louis Gallo

Waail, podner, got some purty senoritas
over in Dodge City
and the Marshal's not too swift.
Tequila by the crate.
Scorch your palms on some hot skin
and nothing much matters,
especially if you're de-ranged.
Glad, sad, easy, mad . . .
all smashed into the great phallic twitch.
I swear if God ain't one eternal hard-on.
Don't know about you
but I'd skedaddle otherwise.
Cause I'm plumb terrified.
Lotsa rattlesnakes round these parts,
some in your brain too,
kind that swallow their own tails.
So don't hand me no crap
I can't bite in half
like the worm in this bottle.

They ran so fast that the hounds couldn't catch 'em . . .
    –Johnny Horton

You feel his breath
scorch your heels
as you duck around a corner
and stop at the lamp post
to catch your own.

WHY IS THERE SOMETHING RATHER THAN NOTHING?

He's not bright,
just persistent, invisible
and no doubt immortal.
Some ancient god
spurned for ugliness.
(Gods should be beautiful?)
Those with frog skin,
hairy lumps or bulging eyes
clump in the shadows
like ruthless afterthoughts.
No piano lessons or petites fours.
They make a go of the streets,
meadows, the heart of the forest,
your bedroom at midnight.
Seize with cold tentacles
and knead until you begin
to resemble them–
as if to snap off one of their own ribs,
whittle and suck for a simulacrum.
Devoid of feeling,
they cannot know–
or know only too well–
the horror they inspire,
the frantic search for exits
and refuge of caves, darkness,
the storming of emergency rooms.

A legless Korean veteran
propped against the wall
of *Naked Girls* on Bourbon Street

says it's like sex with Doom.
You slip a dollar
into his palsied hand
and pick out
one of the miniature American flags
stuck in a slab of Styrofoam.

It's just about Christmas
and the bustled merriment
and autonomic cheer
drop you to your knees
as you embrace the only god
who ever blessed you
with unconditional love.

7

Why did the chicken cross the road?

Damned Buddhist chants
sound like a bunch of geezers
farting together,
some gongs thrown in for effect.
Forgive me if I fly the coop
and wind up in the fifties dive
down lower Decatur
where they still play Jackie Wilson
on the juke.
Know "Please Tell Me Why"?

WHY IS THERE SOMETHING RATHER THAN NOTHING?

Oh, what a song, makes me cringe.
I'm not dumping on Tibet,
I dig the autistic drone
of monks high on austerity.
But sometimes I just need
soul juice spiked with
the angst of profusion,
that is, plenty to lose.
And note,
I avoid the question at hand.
Why cross the road, indeed.
This is not a pipe.
Joke of the century.
To you we're ribs, wings, breasts,
liver & barbecue sauce.
If you're lucky we'll put on a show,
blitz through the yard in circles
looking for our heads.
Suppose I say it's like Childe Roland
hunting the squat dark tower
he knows will undo him.
Half-dead horse collapsing
in the black, dried-up brambles.
Oh, mercy, via dolorosa,
blast out the Sangwa Dupa!
A fucking beak to peck
at darkness rushing you
like tidal waves forged of steel.
You don't want to know

Louis Gallo

why I crossed the road,
why the sight of you coming,
you, stationary ghost of stone,
the road streaking from your frozen tires,
makes me pray for a simple fox.

This is more like it:
cluck, cluck, cluck.
Peep peep.
Cheep, oh, cheep cheep.
Puk puk puk pawkkkkkk.
Heaven is other chickens.
Don't mind that voice of doom,
crappy existentialist, big head.
Thinks he's Sartre Cock.
I'm the real chicken here.
Not one idea since creation.
But that wishbone you crave
is deep inside; got to carve us up
to snap it.
We don't even know
we're crossing the road.
Or that it's a road
or we're chickens
and you've got an ax
in your hands.
So easy, so beautiful,
like never hatching.

WHY IS THERE SOMETHING RATHER THAN NOTHING?

Old blues man:
Chicken say human beans
taste like dem.
Use be a place up Rampart
serve dead human bean
dey find roun town
or sometime dey
stick needles
in lil straw dolls.
Got some lawyez
when dey come slummin'
cuz it cool
& say
vote me & gimmy
all yo money.
I git you five year, top.
Den we tear
like cannibal
at voo doo meat
stuff like crawfish.
Don't taste like no chicken.
Lawyer taste like old puke.
Spit em out fast.

Chicken or egg?
Yin, yang?

Louis Gallo

Where were you before
you were born?
It's in the stars, sweetheart,
eighth house, Jupiter in Mercury,
Mars crossing Uranus, Halley's comet
blitzing through the Oort clouds,
nineteenth phase of the back side
of the moon. Look at those lines
in your hands, and the holes too.
Wow! Such karma the likes
I have not seen since Che Guevara
crossed the Gulf and came to me
in a dream. The texture of his skull
augured no good, and, sure enough,
he died. And let me tell you,
tea leaves or bird excrement,
either way, you're finished.
Call for a free two-minute reading
by one of our friendly psychics
in the comfort of your own home.
Don't linger in your sorry zodiac
when we can deliver you.
In Delphi, the sibyls screamed,
frothed, swatted furies besetting them
like frenzied insects.
In Siberia Shaman buried himself alive
for three days, returned from the dead,
connected his own scattered bones
to align with the vision.
St. Simeon Stylites remained

WHY IS THERE SOMETHING RATHER THAN NOTHING?

atop a ziggurat for thirty years,
his disciples bucketing down the shit.
So let's not toot chickens and eggs
when everything is at stake.
Descend, don't come up
until the fish begin to nibble
your cold, jellied eyes.
You won't care what came first,
or why it crossed,
but you'll know.

8

Who's there?
                —in response to "Knock Knock"

Beast.
    Beast who?
Beastelevation?
    Revelation?
Elevation.
    Aren't they the same?
Open up & see.
    We ain't home. We gave at the office.

Little Anthony.
    Little Anthony who?
Little Anthony and the Imperials.
    I thought you were dead.

We still perform in corrugated sheds out in Westwego.
   Big decline, eh?
Look in the mirror lately? We don't
remember you, but you remember us.
   Wow, this is super. Last time I heard you guys, it was on the radio, I had pimples—and even hair. And you're still kicking!
   It's all you need, one big hit. Sing it over and over, forever. Still waiting for mine.
   Wouldn't be so bad if we didn't have this group arthritis. Won't hold my breath though.
   And the chicks, oldies, man, not the way it was.
Got any advice?
   Can't even reach high notes now without Ludens.
Should I get an agent?
   Just one real inspiration, that's all you need, one
      beautiful, magical moment when you can't stop crying.

Ghost.
   Ghost who?
Ghost in the machine.
   They killed you off. You don't exist.
   Poor dead machine, so many gears, rods and shafts. Junk heap. Don't take it so hard.
   Oh I don't, but shouldn't you?

SETI scans the heavens
for a manicured whisper,
carbonized purr

WHY IS THERE SOMETHING RATHER THAN NOTHING?

or jubilant thump.
Electronic dish sweeping space
like some lonely broom,
terminals recording random hiss
and static, cracked wrinkles
on an old woman's face.
SETI notes a few coincidences,
some unusual blips,
but nothing remotely amiable
in all the sky's dark reach.
SETI mopes, sinks into a funk
so profound that Shaman appears
as if summoned. Shaman
regards the equipment,
shakes a rattle, blows smoke
into the integrated circuitry.
SETI goes wild!
Voices everywhere,
every inch of the universe
ablaze with flaming tongues!
Too many to understand.
What are they saying?
Same as always,
Shaman says, plucking
from the din a single voice
that becomes a white feather
in his fingers.

Louis Gallo

They point out
that since equations require no god,
no soul, not even themselves,
such superfluities do not exist
in any meaningful sense.
Colorful debris, that's about it.
You can scratch figures
onto a board, then disappear;
creation will proceed nicely,
thank you, without consequence.
But every so often
even the figures jitter–
another unwanted infinity,
some new ultraviolet catastrophe
to get them scrambling
back to the lab,
desperate for chalk.
They "re-normalize,"
obliterate us again
and breathe easy,
chameleons taking on a backdrop
until it spits them out
and doves soar from leafless trees
in a shock of radiance.

WHY IS THERE SOMETHING RATHER THAN NOTHING?

9

And what rough beast, its hour come round at last,
Slouches toward Bethlehem to be born?
            —Yeats

She say I da beast,
my ole lady, her bunion swole.
Awright wit me,
worse things a man can be
in dis whorl o misecorderies
like white alligator floatin'
in dat evil swamp
when you go hunt
silly shrimps.
Seen it unner my bed
in a dream
mo hungry den I ever be.
Chew up me, trombone,
whole city wit fine skyscrapes
& church.
Like Ray Chows say,
please don let dis dream come true.
I play song fo you, Jeeze,
if you make nothin' happen
& we all stay same
long long time.

Louis Gallo

Before George retired, he was big at Bayou Utilities.
Bonuses and certificates every year until the day
he dropped dead in the office. That was before computers.
He came home every evening with ledger stains on his fingers.
I'd rub them clean with a little Dr. Tichenor's
and a washcloth. That's why he smelled like peppermint,
my George. He was a good husband,
father, provider and friend
when IT didn't clutch him in its fangs like carrion.
He would lock himself in the cellar–to protect us.
The children and I heard him down there
fling himself against the walls, howl, beg for mercy.
He said IT had assailed him ever since he could remember,
and he didn't even know what it looked like.
It's always coming, he'd say when he was normal,
like the darkest fiend, my own thoughts.
Of course, in those days you kept things private.
No one at Bayou Utilities suspected anything untoward,
though on the day of his funeral
Mrs. Planchette, the secretary,
told me George was the saddest man she'd ever known.
And I swear, every year the earth above him sinks
another inch–as if IT's still after him, trying to dig him up.
And Bobby, our eldest, he creeps around that cellar now.
Sometimes I catch him sniffing the walls
and stabbing a rusty old crowbar into the mud floor.
What will I do with a boy already so touched?
I curse my husband's sperm that was always cold,
and so arid, like dry ice.

WHY IS THERE SOMETHING RATHER THAN NOTHING?

Shaman stands paralyzed
in the howling wilderness,
in the mandala,
as the point of flame
dancing in the dark window
of an ancient temple
zooms toward him,
deafens him with sea rush.
The flame is now a black transparent shadow,
looming, majestic, twice Shaman's size.
Shaman thinks it's his father's spirit
or his lost daughter,
but these comfortable identities
seem wrong, the shadow incensed
at the mistakes.
Shadow takes the form of a man
and looks Shaman over,
studies him.
Shaman fears nothing
but knows the terror will come
and that he will lie trembling
on damp, musty earth.
Shadow recedes slowly back to the temple,
now quivering in the sky like pudding,
and resumes its incessant dance.
Shaman watches for hours
until the vision fades
and wolves howl

Louis Gallo

and a moon
that smells like time
drifts into his nostrils–
not that other moon
glazing our blood with light.

> *Creation Myth from an extinct*
> *people about whom we know nothing*
> *beyond this fragment found*
> *etched in a cave*

The man walking on water
waves back crowds
who crunch popcorn on the banks
as they whoop and whistle
and dare him to try it on one leg.
Two could be a trick, they cry,
two is always a trick.
The man walking on water
slowly lifts a leg and hops around
to show he's no faker.
The people boo and throw Coke cans
and rocks.
One could be another trick!
That man is full of tricks.
We're sick of tricks.
So the man walking on water
lifts his other leg and
crosses both in the lotus position

WHY IS THERE SOMETHING RATHER THAN NOTHING?

above the surface.
The people shake their heads and hiss.
A boring miracle! they shout,
we want impossible miracles!
We want 694 dimensions,
not merely three–or is it four?
And when the floating man obliges,
they hiss and click and shrink
into icy seeds that spill
through countless pinholes
in the porous geography.
The floating man,
helpless without their doubt,
tapers himself out of existence
through a single tear.
And this tear
will someday fluctuate
in a sloppy vacuum.
They will call it god.

10

*If a tree falls, and no one is around
to hear it, does it make a sound?*
        –vox populi

(Contenders:
What, me worry?
        –Alfred E. Neumann

Louis Gallo

What is the sound of one hand clapping?
    —Zen koan popularized by J.D. Salinger

Teen angel, can you hear me?
    —Bobby Vinton

Why is Carl Sagan so lonely?
    —Walker Percy

(1)

Absolutely not, cries Heisenberg,
the wave function has not collapsed.
No collapse, no crème de menthe.
This is what happens
to a photon of light passing
through the celebrated double-slit;
this is that wretched cat
dead and alive at once
(though I am not playing games!);
this is heaven or hell.
Imagine a sea of potential
so aroused that an ear,
an eye or tongue
can instantly reduce it,
your harem, so to speak,
to one sultry, molten wife,
the one you love.

WHY IS THERE SOMETHING RATHER THAN NOTHING?

(2)

Wave function?
Freud approves the phrase.
I take it to mean
the undifferentiated gunk
floating like sleepy wet reptiles
at the bottom
of the mind of the universe.
I told you dreams meant something!
Genius is not energy–
genius is the wolf, Thanatos,
the mons veneris toward which
every phallus arcs.
Double-slit indeed!
You physicists are a nasty lot.
Keep your gropings
strenuously professional
lest they leap out of hand
like the fish that turns into many.

(3)

Dat tree fall wit nobody roun
you bet believe it caboom.
Like my trombone
play itsef, I hear it sing
even if I out somewhere,

down at Cosmo's wit some broad,
gettin' pokechop wit Papa Blue,
licorice stick man, deef
like Helen Kellum.
I hear it when I sleep
& when I dead I will hear it.
Good trombone play itsef,
play even witout itsef,
wit no world, wit nothin'.
Like dat racket of silence
when a tree fall.

Possum wobbles out of the bramble,
follows the trail of sniffing
until he reaches my house again.
Crunchy nuggets in the cat's bowl.
We watch for him all night,
pull back the curtains, make no noise.
Possum knows our vigil,
savors our silence.
He knows we will not harm him,
that in some strange way, we revere him,
take him as an omen of good fortune.
If he misses a night, we sulk, retire out of sorts.
Our cat waits too, stations himself on the porch rocker
and gazes as Possum empties the bowl.
Icon of darkness, with white fur and rat tail,
your lonely zeal has earned our respect.

WHY IS THERE SOMETHING RATHER THAN NOTHING?

We do not want to see you flattened in the street
like so many others frozen by headlights.
We await the moment you turn slowly
to peer into our eyes with serene detachment.
If we had never seen you–
I happened to catch you one night by accident–
would you feast like a guest on our porch
or would an empty bowl signify the usual?
If we in this house suddenly disappeared
and your only witness is a cat
simultaneously dead and alive,
would you remember us as curious ghosts
who summoned your attention briefly
or would you vanish as well,
never having really existed?
Strange communion! Our eyes
and a possum's eyes. Still stranger hungers.
We can, for now, abide only the moment,
still born yet clotted with nuggets
of what will come, what will not–
and they are the same.

Crazy old man,
we took him to see Dr. Johnny
because of the walnut-sized lump
in his neck.
Of course, you expect the worst.
Dr. Johnny took one look

and raised his eyebrows.
"How long have you had this?" he asked—
that most terrible question.
The old man scratched his head, "Had what?"
"The lump. Does it interfere with your speech?"
"Ain't no lump," said the old man.
We expected as much,
denial it's called—the first stage.
"We need a biopsy right away,"
Dr. Johnny advised
as if we were the ones with the lump.
The old man squirmed in his seat.
"No cuts, no needles, nothin' at all.
Ain't no lump."
In the end we had no choice
but to bring him home.
Within the year Dr. Johnny died
of gross malignancy,
and one of us just stopped breathing.
Five years later the old man
sits on the porch rocker with his harmonica.
"Cat's chair," he laughs, "but he's dead too."
The lump has turned into an emerald.
"Ain't no lump," says the old man,
"now vamoose. I'm waiting for Possum."

PART TWO

Westerns

My grandfather stirs condensed milk
into his cup of pekoe tea,
blows on it a while, then pours it
into an earthen saucer and waits
for a wrinkled, slimy membrane to form
on the surface. He slurps it up
and skin-like residue clings to his lips.
I find this disgusting and gag for effect.
"It's the best part, boy," he laughs.
Dad drinks the creamed tea straight
from his cup as do I; too sweet,
I tingle with nausea.

When Miss Kitty appears, Paw starts on me–
"Like that, eh? Watch out you'll get pimples."
He's right, my face flares with blotches
rusted on like iron berries.
I adore Miss Kitty always straining
out of her bodice, her pouty lips,
even the speck of mole on her cheek.
The Marshal seems indifferent
to her thrusts against his chest
when he swings into the saloon
to kill someone, dumb-ass Chester
mewling in the wings.
Wholesome as pound cake,

Louis Gallo

the Marshal grows flat and dense
with boredom, drags himself to the jail.

Paw boasts he hasn't painted
these sooty walls for over thirty years.
And here we huddle, every Friday
and Sunday night, shadowy figments
of ourselves stranded in another era,
while my grandmother, mother and sister
cavort in the sumptuous front parlor.
They aren't allowed, Paw says.
Only men can drink hot tea, watch
cowboy shows and yearn for slivers of breast.

At ten he rises abruptly, snaps off the set
and growls to Dad, "Go home, son, it's late."
He disappears into the bathroom.
Dad and I steer for the parlor,
bright, cheerful and full of laughter;
we refrain from plunging in too eagerly–
a room full of women, after all.
Dad sinks loosely into the sofa
like a crusty varmint groping
into Dodge for water.
Before we leave the house
my grandfather is already dreaming.
Grandma stands behind the screen door
waving her embroidered handkerchief
until we can't see her anymore.
Our tires squeal as Dad takes the corner.

WHY IS THERE SOMETHING RATHER THAN NOTHING?

A stiff Pall Mall hangs from his lip.
Johnny Yuma was a rebel I hum
and warn my sister to stay on her side
of the back seat. She pouts, fidgets.

The Wild West hisses in our Plymouth
and none of us can break free enough
to imagine another, easier future–
certainly not the Marshal, face down
in dirt with a bullet in his back.

Milton, Santayana & Keats

When I have fears that I may cease to see
the beauty in a common moth's wings;
when I considered how my delight was spent
weeks after a random accident . . .
we made the drive to visit our daughters
in their new, first-time apartment
to behold their glittering Christmas tree,
another first for them to erect on their own
and to me an emblem of felicity.

Santayana said: who forgets the past
is doomed to repeat it . . .
but I want it to last,
the jubilant past so concretized,
(without the horrors of course),
unlike the present which does not exist
or the future, too uncertain to call.
I want to walk into that apartment
again and again, forever, I want to foresee
it all, those lights, that perfect tree
and our girls smiling beside it proudly
as I snap the photos, click the shutter
repeatedly, memorialize the instant,
that brief eternity.

Amusement Park

hold on tighter, Marie,
I haven't ridden this Cyclone in years,
last time, Coney Island, before
the Dutch moved out

same thrills of course
but harder to believe—
remember the cotton candy,
the malteds thick as wet cement,
the fried onion rings,
the corn on cobs dripping
with rancid butter,
the stench,
the bruiser who punched
that dog in the jaw
for shitting on the boardwalk?

stay away from that garden,
Marie, with its empty pool
and fluttering rose petals
and mystic light . . .
the archduke is dead,
the country ransacked—

oh, and that boy stranded
high on the Ferris Wheel,

Louis Gallo

how he blew you a kiss
and you blushed
and held firmer my hand?

you can repeat the past
though the past cannot
repeat you, especially you

Archetypes

We bandy about the term as if
we know what we're talking about.
We don't. Nobody does.
Freud said the unconscious mind
is structured like jokes; Jung,
like alchemic transformations.
I say it's structured like chaos, what
that early American "howling wilderness."
Probe that dream you had of driving
along a steep cliff during a mudslide.

Are they endemic to the mind or
to the universe? Did the Ice Man
harken to the moon as I did the other night?
I like to think both, but makes no difference
since we sift the universe through
our very neurons and can't probe it
any other way—that outer extremity.

Jung says one thing, Eliade another
though I like Jung: *there is good reason*
for supposing that the archetypes are the
unconscious images of the instincts themselves,
in other words, that they are patterns
of instinctual behavior." Good—that means
I myself, and you too, we, are our own archetypes.

Louis Gallo

Oh Susana! How I fear the Shadow
but adore the Wise Old Man and the Babe.

Did Bach pluck that motet I listened to
repeatedly as a child out of the cosmos
or did the cosmos feed it into his gray brain
so he could bestow it upon all of us?
The man accosted women in the chapel
on the pipe organ itself. Should we think
less of him for that? I guess so, but that motet
is so beautiful I cringe to hear it. Sacred,
it's sacred.

Excise that banjo out of my heart
so I can plunk out another Doo –Dah.
There's an archetype for you.

Beethoven and Red Beans

I'm on my way to the Blacksburg Kroger
to pick up some Blue Runner red beans
(the only place around here to carry them)
because all the old ladies in my family,
the New Orleans krewe, say they're the best
and they're all fabulous cooks.
You ought to taste Aunt Edna's pound cake
made with twenty sticks of butter
or my grandmother's flan,
my mother's gumbo and cheesecake.

I'm listening to Beethoven's piano sonatas
as I drive, blasted out from a CD.
They can only be described as majestic,
awesome (though the word has been destroyed
by those who find everything awesome)
and, ok, divinely inspired.
I want to buy Beethoven a can of Blue Runner red beans.

Because I'm a Romantic who actually believes
the old notion that we are mere conduits
for what the Muses or God inspire.
Because how else explain such music?
How else could a sorry man like Ludwig
van Beethoven, a miserable wretch really,
how else . . . unless so touched?

Louis Gallo

We're having red beans and rice tonight
with lots of garlic, green peppers and onions.
Then I'm filling up a bowl with leftovers
and setting it on the porch, just in case
Beethoven comes creeping around in the dark
like some emaciated dog.
Ah, culinary sonatas of shrimp and rice
and more secrets than the notes of a piano.

Break

I'm sitting on my front porch
trying to catch a little breeze and shade
having just descended from the back flat roof
where I have been for days scraping weather boards,
applying primer, painting, scrubbing gutter pipes,
cleaning the same pipes, and I'm besmeared
with primer, paint, caulking, gutter slime,
and what a mistake to attempt such a job
when the sun is rising and there is no patch
of shade anywhere, the run relentless
in my eyes, baking my skin, and this happened
just now, moments before writing this,
as I sit in the rocker drinking two bottles
of aqua straightaway, and a blue jay
swoops down onto the banister not three feet
before me and he cocks his head and turns
to stare at me for a good minute
and I stare at him (or her) and he squawks gently
as if to say, what an asshole!
then raises his wings and flies away.

Dream of Cragsmoor

I'm staying with my rich friend
in upstate New York at his stone
robber baron mansion.
We're driving down the mountain
through whorls of fog and mist,
sometimes total white out,
and I can't imagine how he steers
blind.
      We're trying to find supplies
at this dinky little grocery, the only one
in the vicinity, and as I search for
cans of tuna fish, bread, baby Swiss,
yogurt, I see the products on shelves
(what are the odds?) but when I try
to retrieve them, they disappear.
The weird loaf of bread I had dropped
into my basket also vanished.
My friend is impatient, says
the weather is getting worse.
I frantically scan the store
for something to eat, anything
at this point
bur return to the station wagon
with an empty basket,
resigned to starving to death.

WHY IS THERE SOMETHING RATHER THAN NOTHING?

We head back up the mountain
into a swash of black ink
and the vehicle swerves
off a cliff and seems to descend
smoothly forever. I figure,
what the hell, and recall a line
I heard in some cheesy movie:
when things get out of control,
stay calm and go along for the ride.
Could be worse, I laugh,
Everything, even the worst,
could be worse.

Ergo Sum

That's the part that haunts me, has
haunted me for decades, ergo sum,
as it implies that what doesn't think—
say, plants, rocks, water, earth itself—
doesn't exist, and yet we know they exist,
don't we? Dr. Johnson kicking the rock,
for instance—Berkeley refuted, instantly,
and yet . . . if we attribute varied degrees
of consciousness even to plants and rock
and Omnia as would shamans and animists
(those myriad river gods, the Roman lemures)
we might get away with it except that quantum
physics wants to shindig now with the philosophers:

the Copenhagen School, the most Prussian
and conservative (and I stress conservative)
with its impeccable equations stipulating that
(1) either an infinity of worlds co-exists
with the one we think we're in or (2) we, US,
"create" reality by merely observing it, the
participatory business, the latter verified
by something called "the collapse of the wave
function," from Schrodinger, whose cat
figures into all this by being dead and alive
at once and either meets the "true death"
(ah, I miss "True Blood") or the true life
when someone opens the lid. Observes.

WHY IS THERE SOMETHING RATHER THAN NOTHING?

So what to make of all this, let's face it,
preposterous speculation? Descartes,
no fool, saw angels. So did Newton, that
sublime yet paranoid mind. Dr. Johnson,
well, just a good old boy at heart—didn't
realize or care that the rock was mostly
empty space however much it stubbed his toe.
And Schrodinger, how dream up the "collapse"
and then prove it mathematically?
Was that poetry or hallucination or revelation?
Could any of us have thought that one up?
Kant's thing-in-itself turns out to be no-thing
but an infinite (?) field of energy, radiation,
potential . . . and thus we somehow emerge
from it to become US and thereby we observe
part of the energy left behind and, voila,
the world—lamp posts, magnolia trees, the
Tower of Pisa (Pizza?), the shrimp po-boy
I crave.

But we've drifted . . . Rene, back to you:
you forever divided the mind and the body
(though many now say you were utterly wrong),
so, for me, you have made such bestowal
and do I like it or not? Who knows? MWF
I like it . . .but does it imply that when we're not
thinking, say, when asleep or in comas,
we don't exist? That's what you're saying, man,
and it sounds crazier than me here
trying to figure it out, thinking about it,
Cogito, my ass (who observed it to create it?).

Faust

Tell me something I don't know
because my ignorance is vast
as all that dark energy and matter,
ninety-five percent of the universe . . .
95% and we think we're enlightened
in our puny five percent
though even that iota abounds
with millennia of everything we miss
because there's no time to cram
it all into our hollow skulls,
our cracked, miserable brains,
and I am Faust who yearns,
to grasp it all, to knead it
in my fingers, to kiss its lips,
to reduce it all to a simple, easy
plum I can bite into as its juice
seeps down my chin—
so that the enterprise tastes good
for a change, and no one goes home
desolate, and we're God Omniscient,
not the fools we are, so stupid,
ignorant as a slice of white bread.

Free Willy(y)

If as the cosmologists tell us
whatever happens after the initial
singularity (that is, the primeval atom
of the Big Bang) has been pre-determined
by the configurations of space & time
inherent at the beginning
then forget the idea that you "willed"
yourself to take that trip to El Paso
on a Greyhound bus so you could see
Texas in all its arid glory—
you didn't. The Big Bang willed it
along with everything else in its wake
(pun intended). The time you think
you chose to meet Suzy at Café du Monde,
that too, engineered by the quantum mechanics
of the Bang—and it goes for Suzy too.
She had no choice but to apply mauve
eye shadow that morning, though it was
probably evening—some "law" fifteen
billion years ago decided for her.
Best to pretend you know what
you're doing, though, best for Suzy too
because what if you surrender to
the straight jacket of determinism,
what if you comply with what you
can't help complying with? Might

Louis Gallo

as well jump the gun you can't jump
and cry "Geronimo" as you dive off
the cliff in Acapulco into the Pacific
with Suzy clinging to your back.
It's a kind of redemption, an AS IF
of delicious, confectionary hallelujahs.
You might even meet Willy down there.

PART THREE

Glass Booth

They propped her up in a glass booth
that reminded me of that other booth
into which they sequestered Adolph Eichmann
at Nuremberg.

This too was a trial of sorts—they intended
to measure every aspect of her breath,
its density, possible aberration, atomic
fluctuation . . . everything, the measurements
of which appeared graph-like on a computer
attached to the breathing tube,
like an oscilloscope of old, those graphs.

It was a kind of torture and not only for her
but for me also who witnessed her discomfort
and fear. The greater the technology,
the greater the horror, a wise man once said.
But you don't have to be wise
to know that. Witnessing is enough.

Golem

I learned about them from a handbook
of Jewish folklore, they multiplied in my mind
like a phalanx of horrid Chuckies or perhaps
Lilliputians, though the latter had sense enough
to ensnare Gulliver. Vile golden replicas
or pint-sized clay humanoids without spirit
(see Psalms), they abound in the shtetls
of Prague and Warsaw—another species maybe,
unformed raw mud or metal, failed prototypes,
dwarfed, brainless, purposeless, creepy . . .
insects that look like us, swarming about
or solo at the corner of your eye, streaking,
a reminder of the before-you mistakes,
grotesqueries of evolution, the gingerbread man
of *Shrek* crying "Eat me."

Once while driving the interstates at night,
sleepy, beginning to hallucinate, I spotted
them dash across the road and give me
the finger as they fled. I checked into
the nearest Holiday Inn, crashed, dreamed
they marched into the room and siphoned
out my blood into gasoline canisters.
I'm not even Jewish! Nor are they.
Mere reminders that other non-Others,
hangnails of existence, populate the sub-world

WHY IS THERE SOMETHING RATHER THAN NOTHING?

and occasionally cross over—some bizarre
need for homage, acknowledgment, tribute.
Best to lock your doors and station a bottle
of Flit on the bedside table.

I Thought They Had Everything

I once rented out a small portion
of an antique mall in South Carolina
to sell the relics I had accumulated
over the years. Petty cash usually.
A frequent customer, not of my booth
but the main store of expensive stuff,
was this very rich and very beautiful
young blond woman who drove a Jaguar,
her husband a big-shot lawyer around town.
Whenever I spotted her I felt longing—
she had everything and was gorgeous
to boot. Not fair of course but the nature
of desire overlooks injustice . . .

One day the owner informed me that Gina
(let's call her Gina) had hanged herself
from a rafter in her three-car garage.
I was stunned. So much we don't know—
the intricacies of genes and chromosomes,
the status of distant supernovae since
the light from them we behold flared
billions of years ago, the propagation
of DNA everywhere (we share it with
bananas, spiders, baboons, goldfish,
et al.), the leaping of quanta . . .
so much, so little, so omnia.

WHY IS THERE SOMETHING RATHER THAN NOTHING?

And we hear about the other suicides—
say, Robin Williams, Anthony Bourdain,
successful, rich, popular suicides. Why?
Depression we assume since you've got to be
pretty sad to off yourself, right?
I thought we could tally the blessings
against the agonies and determine what
outweighed what. Make such lists,
experts inform us. What is a list?
Scratches on a pad, hieroglyphs.

I see Gina sweep into the store, all smiles,
radiant almost iridescent beauty
subsuming the premises, I see her fondle
a Nippon vase from the fifteenth century,
I see her whip out her checkbook.
I want to know why she killed herself,
she who had everything–
and what is everything?

Ice Wagons

While driving my youngest daughter
somewhere on a curvy, two-lane mountainous road
we found ourselves behind a very old, home-brew
dump wagon that spewed hay and gravel
from its open top. Twenty miles an hour
in a fifty-mph zone. "Damned ice wagons,"
I cried out in frustration. And she, "What's
an ice wagon?" How could she have known?
I remember them as a kid in New Orleans
when literal ice wagons still clogged the streets,
delivering massive blocks of ice here and there
from the Acme Icehouse on Carrollton Avenue.
You could drop your quarter into a slot
and such a block would rumble down the chute;
we wrapped them in towels and got home
in time for the ice cream churn.

I tried to explain to her what I meant
and now whenever we get behind
a real turtle, one of us cries out, "Ice Wagon."
When I asked my students if any of them
knew what an ice wagon was, none of them
registered. Oh, how the past dwindles away
from generation to generation, how the ice
wagons vanish (except of course the slow pokes
we call by that ossified name). Later I heard her

WHY IS THERE SOMETHING RATHER THAN NOTHING?

talking to a friend on her cell phone and
I caught the word "emoji" in passing.
"What's an emoji?" I later asked. She laughed—
"don't you know anything?"
The future catches us off guard. We
ice wagons watch emojis blitz by
as we cruise along almost in reverse.

Inspirations

You take some lines from Rimbaud,
that filthy yet gorgeous teenager
who lured Verlaine from his wife
into weeks of drunken orgies
only to abandon poetry at nineteen
to run guns and capture slaves
in Africa,
soon dying of cancer of the knee.

You take, say, the lines

> *I made up rhymes in dark and filthy places,*
> *And like a lyre I plucked the tired laces*
> *Of my worn-out shoes, one foot beneath my heart.*

and wonder how they apply
because they don't apply
though of course they do, beautifully

because the shoe, the heel and sole,
always transport the heart
even in quicksand

and the heart beats faster,
that staccato lyre,
as you walk, as you pace the earth,

WHY IS THERE SOMETHING RATHER THAN NOTHING?

as you shift from cognita to the other
and defeat geography until

the knees give out, the skin peels
like an onion, and you drown
in what the French call *avillissement*

or the degradation you have always feared
coming your way from the beginning

can't sink any lower, your price goes down
yet you sing and like a potter at the wheel
mold wet ugly clay into a song
or a poem or some objet d'art
worthy of the gods

Traveling

The dream precedes and subsumes
and often precludes reality.
This is what happened as I drove south
to Spartanburg on a dusty leftover road
spotted with fireworks, pottery and peach
cider stands—because, you see,
Carolina and the Civil War, my past,
disappeared from the atlas, wound up
in a different zodiac, whereas I had fired
that first shot in another chronicle
writ by a blind man with tattoos
burned into his eyes—the Hanged Man
upside down—his lips quivering
as he pointed toward a woman
on the horizon, her lips moist and carmine,
her mien mystic, her gaze Byzantine
and sultry, the child in her arms
haloed.

When I crossed the state line
the old colony smoldered in my rear
view, the troops scattered, fallen,
vultures licking clean the entire state.
I drove on, the miles multiplied,
hungry, dull-witted,

WHY IS THERE SOMETHING RATHER THAN NOTHING?

stopped for some scrambled eggs
at a diner in Wyoming
where a man about to lose his mind

thumped the counter with charred fingers
as he muttered a doxology.
I mused therefore upon the righteousness
of delusion and again regretted
the nothing new that squirms under
the ancient sun.

To or Not To

I say, I love thee, Ariadne
but what didn't I say?
what's more important?
what did or didn't you say?

or what I did
what I didn't do

or what I thought
what I didn't think

or what I believed
what I didn't believe

or or or or or or or or

Time as Disease

I once wrote that nostalgia was a disease
whereas I know now that it's merely a symptom
of that greater disease, Time, which, they say,
is a byproduct of the second law of thermodynamics,
as if that explains anything. What about my
or your itch for love as concrete as a blue
Victorian hand-vase, milk glass on the inside,
with an orange aromatic rose rising out of it
like an antenna? What about the molasses
chunks, the sugar cane segments, my father
brought home from Saltifarchia's grocery,
the taste of both lingering in my mind
like the musical note of that Bach motet
I played over and over again on a remote,
childhood phonograph?
Does the mind process music and aromas
in the same vault as words, as experience?
I know too that we need Time for music
to expand, for smells to smell, for words
to signify, for experience to happen.
Otherwise, you're in some Oriental void,
you're stranded on the sub-atomic level
where Time evades the equations altogether.
Who wants to be frozen in either?
Wallace, I won't agree that death is the mother
of beauty, I refuse to, but you've got a point.

Louis Gallo

Rather, Time is the mother of beauty,
Time, our terminal disease, imagine . . .
the grotesque irony. How long can we
hang in, sniffing that rose, chewing that
molasses, gasping to music so beautiful
we want to live forever, drag it out as the
expanding universe races away from
one wonder into another.
And Time, that mother, is contagious.
We're all infected.
Even as some of us wind up like that Ice
Man, fossilized on a glacier, his sack
of seeds, herbs and tools still ready to go.

Meem's House

A mosquito hums daintily as a tiny violin
because Paw forgot to patch the screen door.

Meem hobbles away to the kitchen with the last platter.
Mom sweeps off the linen tablecloth and folds it up.

My sister has disappeared with the women.
Dad and Paw settle down in the TV room to watch
Sugar Ray.

I sit at the table that Paw made
with his hands and rub its surface.

Somehow I know this table will survive,
that it will wind up in either my house
or my sister's. Its grain is cool, smooth.

I am ready for Meem to finish the dishes
and return and hoist me onto her lap as we read
another section the Encyclopedia Britannica.
Dinosaurs were last week.

I imagine a candle fluttering at the center of the table.
I want a honeysuckled breeze to waft through the screen door.

I want Uncle Achille to open that door
on his Friday night visits,

Louis Gallo

and I want to hear its spring squawk,
that familiar, grating honk.

I already knew then what it would
come to all these years later,
that the sounds and scents of that room would stay.

Of course I didn't know. What am I saying?
How could I have guessed, I a mere child?

But the lace curtains on the windows flutter,
the green French shutters remain paralyzed in place,
the grain of the table still brushes against my palm
as I rub it in ever widening circles.

The Thing

When you first get the thing
in all its pristine virginity
you can't keep your hands off of it
and display it proudly in the best
room of your house. After a while
the thing grows a bit dull
and you move it into a lesser room
where after another while
it gathers some dust
which you wipe off
and while you're at it
move the thing to an obscure shelf
and though you still revere
the thing you sort of forget
where it is until the day
you find it somewhat shrunken
and again shrouded with dust
so you pack an attic box
and wrap the thing in newspaper
and place it gently within
along with other maybe older
things and you carry the box
up the stairs to the dark attic
and stack it atop another box
and proceed to forget about
the thing until fifteen years later

Louis Gallo

when unloading excess
you open the box and realize
you have had forgotten the thing
for good but you polish it up
make it near pristine once more
and display it again in the best room
of the house because it is so
beautiful and now venerable
and how can you not look at it
and touch it and smile
a few more times.

The Male Member

I know what you're thinking
but that's not what this poem is about.
So go away.
I happen to be the sole male member
of a poetry writing group
and of course that privilege
is double-edged.
There's Jill who thinks women alone
write the best stuff—
I ask, Shakespeare? Donne? Keats?
No matter, Jill insists
so I agree, women alone.
Then Katie who suspects that male
poets are either openly or latently gay.
Uh, Keats and Fanny, Petrarch and Laura,
Byron and . . . no, forget Byron.
Ok, Katie, you're probably right.
And Jeannie, oh Jeannie, light my fire,
Jeannie . . . but she's through with men,
women too, because one more heartbreak
and she will slit her wrists.
Don't die Jeannie, call me, I have band aids.
And Justine, she writes poems
that make you weep, poems that solder
the words into your mind, poems
that change the universe . . .

there are a few more who come and go
but I am steadfast, I attend each meeting
and they berate my poems
because they suck, as Justine scoffs,
and she's right though not all of them
suck, only most.
Like this one.
Nevertheless, a group of male poets
is unthinkable—Go, team, go—
wait, no, a group of male poets
would be identical to my group
of female poets—only with different members.

You

there was nothing like you
in Toledo or all of Oklahoma
nothing in the soybean fields
and Chisholm trails
nothing in Plymouth
and the ruins of Jamestown
you came along sui generis
in a fire cloud, a typhoon,
you blazed in, you rained in,
an inferno and tidal wave
you swept me away
in a maelstrom of delight,
you soothed me down,
up, in all directions,
latitude, longitude,
you, Equator, the horizon

The Bearable Heaviness of Being

for Milan Kundera

Heavy the proton, heavy the iron, heavy
the anvil, heavy the earth, heavy the soul,
heavy heaven . . . why something rather
than nothing? Nothing, the heaviest.
Strap on your backpack and streak out
for El Dorado and the heavy bones of
countless conquistadors. Look,
a heavy bird dropping out of the sky,
crashes, another crater, Tunguska,
so much (mulch) has happened!
Pleistocene and all the others,
though, who remembers or cares?
Hey, all we can do to get through a day,
so much mass and inertia each moment,
not to mention vector and velocity
and what happens to a light beam
gliding through that double slit.

I once frequented a bar in New Orleans
called the Abbey, on Decatur Street.
All the art farts, drunk and depressed,
until one night a biker gang roared in
and my friend tackled their chieftain
and pinned him to the floor.
Then that supper with Vera at some joint

WHY IS THERE SOMETHING RATHER THAN NOTHING?

on Bourbon Street when the rat
fell out of a palm tree onto our table.
Or at Corrine Dunbar's on St. Charles
when we drank so many vodka martinis
we stumbled out of the place
into a cab. So much to remember,
the past is so heavy, the past at
critical mass, no elasticity except
in the imagination. I remember it all.
I was in Thebes, Jericho, Ur, that latter
the heaviest of all, the ever-present origin,
the anchor, as entire civilizations
swept forth in a flood of creation,
washed over the planet like suds
and evaporated into the heavy stars.

The Wheel

My mother is losing her memory
and I fear that when it erases itself
entirely, as happened with her sister
years ago, I fear that much of my memory
will also disappear into the diaphanous mists
and gauzy fog of miasma.
For much of her memory is my memory
and much of my identity is her memory
and therefore I wonder what this next
covered wagon will drag with it—
whose visions and dreams, what bakeries
and groceries, church pews and cul de sacs.

If my mother sometimes fights
the current, attempts another backstroke,
most of the time she seems content,
even happy (as did her sister)
in the new translucence, the cloud
of unknowing that is all her knowing,
her own realm, impenetrable to me
or anyone else. Once fully enshrouded
I would like to think that she will finally
mother herself into a new and wiser
childhood, a kind of endless playground
with carousels and Ferris wheels and

WHY IS THERE SOMETHING RATHER THAN NOTHING?

spinning saucers, where peacocks roam,
and fauns, bunnies, doves and dogs,
that she will somehow know that we,
now also her parents, watch over her
as she climbs the steps once more
to board an easy, gentle wheel
for another ride that may last
another kind of forever.

The Arrow of Time

I saw the straight arrow of time
streak before me, a blazing flame
with serrated forks or tongues
igniting the darkness, and I
saw that each fork demarcated
a moment then a day, month, year,
each of which signified a duty,
an imperative, a mission, and
to veer meant disgrace, ruin, failure,
these glowing notches of accomplishment
and triumph . . .but as if upon
an instant sudden I heard music,
sweet yet dolorous, enchanting
violins, harps, flutes, dulcimers,
a temptation I could not resist
even at the utmost peril, damnation,
and I so veered, stopped to listen,
broke my bones, lacerated my skin
on those barbed tongues
which screeched infamy, sedition
because I could not resist its lure
and I knew the tongues bore lies,
that they hated such delicious diversion
from the prescribed arrow, its abstract
fire and its gnarled, skeletal claws,
but I chose to listen and behind me now

WHY IS THERE SOMETHING RATHER THAN NOTHING?

the ashen, smoldering remnants
of rash irresponsibility, incomplete
tasks, wasted time, a deluge
of wasted time that had no power
to smother that arrow of fire . . .
because the music mesmerized me,
seduced me, tantalized me,
made me unwise.

The Others

Not the ones you have known and loved
from the beginning as if fused in historic symbiosis

but those others, some who blossom in the mind's
horticulture as lotus petals and others acrid cigar stubs

those you may have spotted once thirty years ago,
say, a flare of burnished hair in the passing convertible

or the snarl of that legless man propped upon a dolly
wheeling himself up Bourbon Street with his hands

or the one slumped over his steering wheel drenched
in sweat or a girl hula-hooping in Central Park,

a cigarette hanging from her lower lip, a stalactite
of desire . . .

the ones who persist, nameless, vanished forever
yet memorialized for no reason you can discern

perhaps merely as reminders of what might have been,
the horrors and the blessings, had not time directed

your arrow elsewhere . . . ah, the beauty who smiled
bounteously, near the produce, in Kroger, ages ago

Ornate Jewelry Boxes

One of my jobs, to mix the crystals with water
in an electric heating pot by DeVilbiss,
only enough liquid to turn the muck
into a viscous, foul-smelling glue,

horse bones, my father said, hold true
the oak we clamped together then unclamped,
joints you couldn't dislodge with a hammer.

They sent the crystals in sacks from Alabama
and I would stir the boiling water in
and sniff the fetid steam that festooned from
the surface as it bubbled and hissed

and choke not merely because it stunk.
I thought about the horses galloping
across fields, between trees, now
planed to slender boards we fused together

to make jewelry boxes for someone's mother,
daughter or some other who just might hear,
if only faintly, the clop of hooves
or sense an oak's wind-sweet breath.

Song of a Man on the Verge

These days I find myself doing a lot of nothing,
and by nothing I don't mean
a plunge into the sumptuous void
of Oriental suction (an easy osmosis
I would welcome), no sir,
the kind of nothing that buzzes, clinks,
hisses and bongs, a havoc of spirit and soul
that spits itself onto the mirror
and splatters.

Buttons hang by mere threads, cuffs frayed.
Tiny frantic shadows scurry across my face.
It's a kind of endurance, exhilaration,
teetering on the edge of some empty vault.
If I've learned one thing about Hawaii,
peace of mind and the space between objects,
it's that geography and time gnaw the same bone.

But we're not fully wayward here, not yet.
Verging has its specific beauty, a spray, yes,
the exquisite blueprint of haze, blur and smudge,
those visible shenanigans.
This is how we live and die, refusing to budge
from what it's come to,
not what has or might have been or will be,
but the eon lodged between tick and tock.
the knowing and the knowing not.

Outer Space

Pascal gasped in horror at the dark,
lonely, open spaces of the universe—
as do I. You couldn't pay me enough
to cruise in a rocket to the moon or Mars
or any other place out there.

I once saw a movie about an astronaut
who died aboard his craft somewhere
far from Earth. The crew wrapped him up
in mummy bandages and shot him out
of a depressurized cabin into outer space—
and we, the moviegoers, watched as that
grim mummy floated away eternally.

I saw it as a kid, and the scene haunts
me to this day. I'm Virgo. I like my feet
planted firmly on the ground, or on sand,
or the redolent, ancient bricks of Bayou Road.
I'd rather take my chances in the sea
than someplace where our planet takes
the form of a distant star. Chilling!

I want to touch the barks of trees,
sniff flowers, fork my fingers in the dirt,
stroll in surf. I like where I am
and whether in the future as corpse
or ashes in an urn plan to stay:
Terra Cognita—I'll send you a postcard:
WISH YOU WERE HERE!

PART FOUR

Overheard

A hunched ancient man and younger woman,
presumably his daughter, herself not so young,
grope out of the Minute Clinic, and loudly
she asks, "Did they take out your catheter?"
And he, cupping his ear with palsied fingers,
says, "Eh?"
She repeats the question, louder than before.

I am waiting outside the ice cream parlor next door
for my daughter to emerge beaming with a cup
of chocolate swirl frozen yogurt.

The woman drives the old man away,
his head flopped over the front seat rest,
his mouth agape.

I liken the sweet yogurt treat against a world
of catheters and dismay. Only a matter of years,
I think, yet not always. I know a boy stuck
in his wheelchair practically since birth—
afflicted with a neurological viper.

I quickly pray that my daughter returns,
delighted, with a plastic spoon, and a smile,
that the old man feels no remorse or pain,
that my child never need to ask such questions.

Pelicans

       accompanied by slow bluegrass

you're down in Cutoff, Louisiana
with a girl you crave
and you stop for shrimp po-boys
in this shack with a reputation
and, yes, so delicious
with a chilled bottle of Dixie

she came with a camera
and shot you leaning on a piling
where squatted a pelican
and then you lounged on the back seat
of the van with her on your lap
smoking a joint of two

you start to unbutton her blouse
because everything seems right
but she brushes your hand aside
and giggles and you know what
that means so you give up
though you don't get it

another pelican swoops down
onto the hood and stares you down,
the girl now asleep, drunk maybe,
dreaming of the best po-boy she ever had

WHY IS THERE SOMETHING RATHER THAN NOTHING?

with exactly the correct blend
of horse radish—how do they
concoct it so perfectly?

but of course you remain bleak
because no po-boy however fine
tastes delicious as that girl's lips
and soon you never see her again
and you're far away now
in a place where no pelican flies

no Christ-like pelican to feed
the young with her own blood

People

Some people you've known all your life
not because you've known them all your life
but because the instant you meet, you, as they say,
"click," though I prefer the term resonate.
Your wave functions synchronize, instantly,
and instantly you know you've known them
forever, though you met only an hour ago,
a kind of osmosis.
                      I like to think that you see
part of yourself there in the Other and vice-versa.
I like to think that maybe some formerly conjoined
but now separated strands of DNA recognize each other,
that somewhere back then you shared an ancestor,
and upon meeting again they cry "Eureka!"

And what about the vast, multitudinous collective Other,
those you forget immediately or fast enough,
those who fade into your misty mid-region of Weir.
They too click with someone somewhere;
they too resonate, clasp their wave-functional hands,
share an ancestor, some Lucy, some Eve, some Sargon.
But you don't recognize them, nor they you—
There is no convergence, no reunion, no communion.
Just "have a nice day" and be on your separate ways,
goodbye, hardly got to know ye, don't want to know ye.

Raccoon

I stepped onto the deck a few nights ago
to gaze at the new moon's gauzy glow
but before I could lift my head to the sky
I stood face to face with a pair of eyes
that locked me into place, and it too
at barely three feet, my shoes glued
to the boards fast in place.

A raccoon, gorgeous, wild and large—
it had strewn garbage from the can
all over the place. It looked at me
then fled without a trace.
But I held fast and yearned for its return.
Not often do you peer into darkness
and discern something other than darkness
itself, the sight of eyes upon you
stranded in the night.

Descartes Thrives

We really don't believe that we
are one with our bodies.
Mind/body dualism lives on.
The minute we say "my brain"
or "my heart" we quarantine ourselves
from these organs.
My is the key,

Who is the "my" that possesses?
Yeats said we are fastened
to dying animals.
So who is the "we"?
Soul? Spirit? Aura?
Something to live on perpetually,
the protein of religion.
Otherwise we're chunks of meat,
Spleen, liver, intestines, kidneys . . .
We don't want to be chunks of meat!
Too disgusting, fetid, ephemeral.
The vulture does not dine on me, however.
How does consciousness transcend
the butcher shop?

Why? A big mistake—or maybe
evolution is taking us on a road trip
beyond hamburger. Someday, surely.

WHY IS THERE SOMETHING RATHER THAN NOTHING?

But too late for us. Goodbye.
Diogenes instructed his disciples
to toss his corpse into a ditch
to feed the dogs.
His body, not Diogenes.
Diogenes went elsewhere.
Bye Diogenes, bye everyone.
Lots of human slop seeping
into the planet.
What Walt wrote about in "This Compost."
But Walt dug it, said the soul was the body.
Bye Walt.

Same Ole

Ever feel you're getting nowhere
because the usual exigencies—mailing out bills,
draping your shirts on hangers, scrubbing the toilet,
deciding what to eat tonight (you know, the usual
everyday)–hold you back so that instead of heading
for Yuma to find the woman in the pill box hat
who threatened to kill you on a Greyhound bus
en route to San Francisco (when you first read Marquez)
or sneaking over to the Yucatan with Gretchen
from Bavaria, instead of something new and thrilling
you find yourself holed up in the house vacuuming
debris from the carpet or scrubbing the hardened
remains of tomato sauce from a pot or spraying
spiders? Ever want to slide behind the wheel
and just drive until the gas runs out—even it you're
stranded in Beeville, Texas, at one hundred degrees
in the shade, no bills, no pesos, no nothing, just
you in a damp sombrero, scampering after a gila moster
because you're hungry and will eat anything—
cactus tastes pretty good once you pull out the spikes.
The phone messages accrue but you don't want to talk
to anybody, especially that chirpy one who informs
you that you've won a grand cruise to Somalia.
She keeps calling, so does BankAmerica with news
of better interest rate (fifty percent, not eighty),
ever want to smash the land line with that sledge

WHY IS THERE SOMETHING RATHER THAN NOTHING?

hammer out in the shed—and toss the cell into
some lagoon in Barataria? Why is it all too much?
A surgeon general once reported that it's not the big
stuff that exponentializes stress—divorce, deaths
of friends, the house collapsing—it's the accumulation
of micro-horrors, scrubbing that spaghetti sauce
from the pot for the thousandth time, raking
the half dead lawn, the usual . . . nice to embark
on something new — "Lady in pill box hat, why'd
you threaten to kill me? Can I buy you a drink?"
Gretchen from Bavaria, meet me not in Yucatan
but Colorado Springs, you know, for the medicinal pot.
Otherwise, I'm not game for much these days—
that sauce, now petrified, ineradicable:
I refuse to scrub it away one more time.

Some Punctuation Marks

Quotation marks are barbarous,
chains around some bird's wing
Clunkers they are, and ugly.
BUT: the alternative is confusion,
chaos, never knowing who's saying what
without pain.

Dashes, how I love dashes,
those kisses between one set of lips
and the other.

Commas, little motes, rice kernels,
bird seed, Spunkey the Monkey
everywhere—but you must learn
when to get rid of most of them
and which are girders.

Periods. Too finale for me, they
scare me. Terminal. Whah!
Now I lay me down to sleep.

Exclamation points—I mean business,
Horatio! Get thee to a nunnery!
Go sexual intercourse yourself!

Ellipses—for gaping; flimsy bridges
disguising the trash between,

WHY IS THERE SOMETHING RATHER THAN NOTHING?

the noise, the whatever you don't want
anyone to know.

Colon: ah, the promise beyond—
But don't forget your colonoscopy.
Terrible verbal coincidence
yet useful, again, for clarity.

Semi-colons—technically to fuse
two independent clauses
which is why I don't like them.
The king died; the queen cried.
Looks weird, avoid them.

Parentheses—another lover of mine,
all those little nothings you want in
but don't really belong, well, they
belong somewhere else
but you can't resist.

Natural Selection

Some stand brazenly in the mind
like pickets of a long, winding fence
the beginning obscure, the end
nowhere yet in sight.
The pickets seem endless
though some have disintegrated
as if dissolving into the ground
from which they once rose.
I was perusing one of my journals
from way back and came across the name
of a young woman with whom,
as recorded over more than several pages
and occupying much of its volume
(her name chronicled throughout)
I once caroused.
I cannot remember her at all now
however tightly I strain and squeeze
the old brain for its memory-blood. . .
it's as if she never existed, survives
merely as an archeological relic.
Others you might have met only
in passing or communed with
sporadically still flare foremost—
pickets ablaze, a psychic Rushmore.
That kid from grammar school,
Richard Z., your great friend

WHY IS THERE SOMETHING RATHER THAN NOTHING?

for a month or so before he moved
out of town with his family—
a speck of timescape, a minor
grace note in the symphony . . .
but there he registers, sturdily,
or that girl who paused at the Jazz Fest—
this decades ago—to wink and smile,
whose name you never knew, spotted
for a split second, and poof!, gone
forever. She too embedded firmly
in the pantheon, indelible.
What ignites the mind and why?
Why do some golden ingots vanish
and others, mere tin or lead, persist?
What Darwin dare decipher the whole
and sixteenth notes of a score, the
loose thread and the tapestry?
Spontaneous Overflow

I heard about a disorder symptomized
by sudden bouts or weeping or laughing
for apparently no sound or specific reason.
It's regarded as a psychiatric condition.
Well, lately I find myself overflowing
spontaneously with such bouts because
everything is so fucking beautiful—
the crepe myrtle blossoms in my back yard
from a sprig I planted years ago from
my mother's tree in New Orleans, the
hummingbird that hovers before me

Louis Gallo

as I slouch on the deck, its wings frenzied
with jazz, the black coffee I swallow
and savor, the wife and children I love,
Cinnamon accepting daintily and joyously
a ridiculous Vanilla Wafer from my fingers—
no need for the jagged Rockies or venerable
Swiss Alps, no comets in the sky, no full
eclipses of the universe, no supernovae . . .
merely the everyday lovelies, those daffodils
fluttering and dancing in the breeze, the
rainbow, the ladybug foraging through
the hairs on my arm . . . nothing special,
but of course, special enough to engender
tears of wonder and exultation or maybe
laughter because you had missed it all
in that previous life you called your life.

Superstition

Superstition is the homespun philosophy
of the masses spawned by dubious
entanglements of cause and effect
and spurious inductive and deductive
leaps, the wreckage of Aristotle,
who, as Stevens put it, is a skeleton.

Yet I, the massiest of men, remain
superstitious as the women
and some of the men of my family.
I trust them more than any logician
or syllogism and its freaky triad:
I refuse to walk under a ladder,
cringe when a black cat crosses my path,
avoid cracks in the sidewalk.
And what about that flock swooping low
over your house? Or the single bird?
And the shriek of an owl at midnight?

Re-consider Yorick, Horatio—he taught me
that all men are mortal, that Socrates, a man,
is mortal, that ergo Socrates is dead.
Look where it got him, a dusty skull in my palm.
Where's the saltshaker? A few grains
over the shoulder. Don't gaze into that

mirror—see its hairline right between the eyes?
The rational mind reduces reality
to a shriveled, eunuched vestige of itself.
But magic, ah, the wishbone in your chicken,
the voodoo in your broth.

Access Denied

I got here by mistake. I don't want in.
It was never in the cards, I refuse
as I would refuse gravity, if I could,
and the heat death and dark energy,
entropy, black holes, whatever goes wrong.

I'd chuck the body itself with all its
sacs and ducts and nodes, the weak links;
and the mind, I'd kick that clown in the ass
if I could.
Don't think I can, Don't think I can.
The little engine that couldn't,
pleased to meet you,
no wonder we de-rail, swerve into imbroglio.

As if the tracks ever lead to someplace
we want to go, like Acapulco,
the trees verdigris and swollen
with fruit. Here at the outpost
it's one powdery foundation after another.
That's how long it's been. Powder,
that queer state between solid and gas.
All you can do to push another button
and remain permanently out.
Access, just another orifice with airs.

Don't Forget to Dance

I'm listening to "Don't Forget to Dance"
by the Kinks on my iPod as I pace beneath
the weeping willow outside Young Hall
waiting for my class to begin. Young Hall,
named aptly, for the building abounds
with a collective youth that remains youth
year after year as I trod the path of Tithonus.

I'm still listening to the mellow, fluid
melancholy of Ray Davies as he sings,

And when they ask me how you dance
I'll say that you dance real close.

I unplug the earpiece and step into the room.

What amazes me about these young ones
is that they too listen, not to Ray who
crooned before their time, but to me, proto-Tithonus . . .
they seem eager to hear what I have to say.
They would prefer not to listen I assume
since it's not cool to hang onto the words
of someone who must seem ancient
and yet something in their cores must remind
them that the ancient does indeed know something
they don't—

WHY IS THERE SOMETHING RATHER THAN NOTHING?

not that they want to know,
not that they would concur or even believe
any of it. What compels them is their
lack of footing and bewilderment
at having been thrust into a chaotic melee
for which they are still not prepared,
floundering in the uncertainty of how to proceed,
seeking clues, gauging their raw instincts
against the "wisdom" of another who traverses
the same road though closer to the finish line
and who surely must have learned
something useful along the way.

What I don't tell them is that I haven't learned
a thing . . . well, of course I have, but no
magic that will help them navigate.
It's mere groping, beginning to end, I suspect
until one's final breath. So I babble and I too
listen to them, hoping they can teach me
something I need and yearn to know.
And when one up front asks what's my best
advice, I pause, forefinger to temple
and croak (for I cannot sing), *Don't forget to dance . . . .*
something, I add, *I forgot to do. How I miss Aurora.*

For I am not the prisoner in Plato's cave
who breaks free to stare into the blinding light
of the sun. I prefer the insight of shadows.

Technology

On the interstate a flatbed truck
loaded with a monstrous, ugly machine
or something like a machine—
passed me at a ridiculous speed
and it occurred to me that if women
ruled the world, no such monstrosity
would exist. Or am I romanticizing?
I don't think women would have invented
jet bomber consoles, not because
they couldn't but because the nature
of such consoles is repugnant
to human nature.
I know I'm a Luddite at heart,
hypocritical enough considering
I indulge in as much technology
as anyone else . . .
but enough is enough.
I imagine the pre-technological
Neanderthals lazing about
smoking joints and picking flowers,
the Ur-hippies, and I envy that
paradisiacal condition, though
surely I am romanticizing.
But the more "advanced" homo sapiens,
that is US, did eventually wipe them out.
Thus the Iron Age advanced toward

WHY IS THERE SOMETHING RATHER THAN NOTHING?

the digital age and now microchips
govern the bomber consoles.
Do I envy the Amish with their horse
and buggies? No. And yet I suspect
less mental illness in their communities.
Do I romanticize? The greater
the technology, the greater the horror,
a wise man once said.
Oh but I do so love word processing
and GPS and Netflix . . .
hypocritical romantic that I am.

Thales

this the Ionian who claimed
that everything was made of water
(Heraclitus vouched for fire)

but if water we must take into account
condensation, evaporation & carbonation
all three of which have always
intrigued me

don't you know people who condense,
who smear themselves all over
a surface
or those who merely evaporate?

carbonation—a slightly different deal
since it involves gas
(and there was another Ionian
who made that claim for everything)

but those who carbonate
rather than evaporate
man, they go out in style
all those sizzling bubbles
and hiss
what razzmatazz!
what crazy style!

WHY IS THERE SOMETHING RATHER THAN NOTHING?

but really
I like the fiery angle too—
and they say Heraclitus
was a most disagreeable man

The Book and Its Cover

Her emotional range limited itself
to "I'm so pleased" and "I'm so frustrated"
as if digitally programmed between
the 1 of modest heaven and the 2 of
equally bland hell. I often hunched
that she was some sort of machine,
a robot of tepid response. When her
father died she sighed forlornly "I'm
so frustrated" whereas when our father
died my sister and I hugged each other
and howled like peasants on the bank
of Bayou St. John across from Hotel Dieu,
where he lay, swollen and inert.

Give her a pair of tweezers for Christmas—
"I'm so pleased"; a million bucks–"I'm
so pleased." She did however daydream
all the time about finding a pot of gold
at the end of the rainbow, literally, that
was the default dream. And yet, as if
to nullify digitalization, she could erupt
in paroxysms of violence–like when she
tried to bash in my skull with a heavy
earthen vase or when she colluded with
legal human Corruption to abduct a child.

WHY IS THERE SOMETHING RATHER THAN NOTHING?

Here's the thing: she was so beautiful
we were all duped into Platonic confusion:
the Beautiful and the Good, synonymous.
The dust jackets of books should be plain,
unadorned, imageless—like those old French
literary paperbacks of the seventies—
so as not to deceive readers who seek
la crème. Check out the embossed, glossy
covers of romance novels—the gorgeous
heroine with windswept chestnut hair
gazing at Atlanta as it burns and smolders.

Then try reading that book beyond, say, its
fifth page as an exercise in exquisite boredom.
Oh, John, you fused Truth and Beauty,
but it ain't so, unless by those terms
you imagined qualities most of us are too
unrefined or dense to grasp.
In a world I might create evil would resemble
the Nosferatu of old, and kindness, love
and truth, Aphrodite. Simple, eh?

Surprised by Beauty in Brutality

Walking from one end of the house to the other
I passed an empty living room, the tv blasting out
a glorious rendition of "God Save the Queen"—
a full orchestra and lead singer, "the dark tenor,"
masked with blackface. Then he sang, with
full accompaniment, the Ukrainian national anthem.
Both songs brought moisture to my eyes.
I assumed some new atrocity had occurred.
But no—the music opened a prize fight,
the Heavyweight Championship of the World
starring Tyson Fury (named after Mike Tyson)
and Vladimir Klitschko, the long-lived, reigning
champion, both, oddly, white men.

The arena, in Dusseldorf, was splendid, brilliant,
clean, arrayed with light beams from every direction.
How could I not think of Charles Bukowski
escorting his whores to boxing matches?
But this arena sparkled with money, class,
aristocratic demeanor, the audience women
all beautiful and ritzy. So I thought of Roman
gladiators competing beneath the emperor's eyes.
I sat down to watch the twelve-round fight,
one of the most boring matches I've ever seen,
not that I've seen many, save for those of Cassius
Clay way back, when I watched religiously.

WHY IS THERE SOMETHING RATHER THAN NOTHING?

So how could I not think of those days
decades ago when my dad, grandfather and I
sat in a darkened room on Miro Street
gazing at the black and white figures jabbing
at each other, the varied Sugar Rays.
No women allowed in that room. They
stayed up in the front room listening to music
and chatting and laughing.

Tyson Fury won the fight almost by default
since Vladimir hardly got in a punch.
Nor did Tyson. They merely danced around
the ring and held on to each other more
than they fought. The referee constantly
broke them up. So how could I not think
of love? The refinement of brutality,
that beauty prancing around holding up signs
signifying the round number.
Twelve of them, sweat, Vladimir with blood
dripping from his temples, Tyson, a giant,
foxtrotting between the ropes.
So how could I not think of Boston and Paris
and all the other savageries
and why we have become what we are?

PART FIVE

The Desire of Persistence

I'm at Trader Joe's seeking the turkey
or chicken canned chili and the nut butter
composed of ten different nuts—pistachios,
too, I hope—and the blueberry scones,
anything that won't melt on the drive home
over Fancy Gap. Cathy and the girls are down
the street at Pet Smart buying some new toys
for Cinnamon, back at the apartment, in her crate
so she won't eat something that would choke her
or chew on wires and electrocute herself.
She cried bitterly when we left. Isn't that always
the way—something to constrain you, assure
displeasure? So it is with dogs—they like
being with you, licking you, nibbling your fingers,
stuff you wouldn't do with just anybody.

Look, up the aisle, a girl in hot pants
and Minnie Mouse mask fiddling with
the mushrooms, fondling the radishes.
It must be Halloween. Have I lost track
of time again? Isn't is June? The month,
I mean, not the girl, though she looks like
a June or May or April, Augusta maybe,
but not October. Who would name a
daughter October? Though I think I read
somewhere that Christian Fletcher (or is it

Louis Gallo

Fletcher Christian) once safely stationed
on Pitcairn Island, far from the rageful eyes
of Captain Bligh, named a son Thursday October
something (maybe it was Tuesday) another
girl's name, like Tuesday Weld, though maybe
I'm wrong. You can look it up. I won't, not again.
I'm finished with looking up. Relying on the
inaccurate, fragile, unreliable memory now,
Mnemosyne, my delicate Muse.

Help me, then, Muse, correct the record,
because I think consciousness is the wave function
of our meaty brains, which means it can collapse
at any random moment into whatever
you're looking for or not looking for.

When?

When did the rational mind arise
out of the bog of fanastical magical thinking,
rationality, the key to syllogisms, dialectics,
digital technology, the postulation of quarks?
All men are dogs. Socrates is a man.
Therefore Socrates is a dog.
Terrence, this is stupid stuff, and all that.
By the way, before proceeding, I like
the irrational, magical, superstitious,
feminine, dark mind that D. H. Lawrence
and Nietzsche celebrate—no poetry or
music out of rationality, no hocus pocus.
I once detected the shift in Sophocles,
Oedipus Rex to be specific—but that
was long ago and I've forgotten the details.
Some say Plato with the cave allegory,
the prisoner breaking free to squint
at the blinding light of reason.
Reason gives us Hiroshima, Auschwitz,
heinous capitalism . . . and no doubt
much good as well, but can we balance
out in favor of one or the other?

After all, consider slave labor in Egypt
to build a pyramid for Tut and his doodads.
Nevertheless, if I had to choose

I'd stick with poetry and music and
toss my cell phone into the peat bog.
Because poetry and music make me feel
good whereas my cell phone does not.
Anything to feel better, right?
The real Eden still blossoms in childhood;
the expulsion, closing in on the adult
around age seven when the doomed child
begins to grasp abstractions.
No ideas but in things.
This anvil or banana (no anti-anvil,
no anti-banana) versus deceptive clouds
like Justice, Honor, Virtue and alas,
even Love and its monstrous ally, Hate.

One of my daughter's first word
was "apple," and when I heard her
speak it, I wept. Apple of discord.
Before that it was all glorious babble
that sounded a lot like poetry to me
albeit in a private, mystic language.
The unexamined life not worth living?
I love you Mr. Socrates but that dictum
set us astray with no runaway ramp,
no brakes, no GPS of return.
Abracadabra.

Why Girls Should Not Eat Meat

Flakey white fish will pass, but not
raw sushi (yuk, salmonella) or black-veined
shrimp and especially not thick, oily
slabs of beef or pork (the worst) . . .
why? Think me sexist if you will
but in my time I've helped produce
four daughters (which beats King Lear)
and thus regard myself as part girl.
Just want to tenderize the world a bit,
make it more aromatic and delicate,
exile barbarous males who would
chomp on live cows if they could.
I call it romantic, not patriarchal.
Where's the nearest matriarchy—
I want honorary membership given
my DNA heritage. Let's nibble flowers
together, sisters—but ok maybe a
hamburger or two when the iron
get a little low. I've probably had
maybe twelve, if that, in the last
twenty years, if that, if that.
I once consumed lamb steak
in a Chicago Greek restaurant
and threw up for a week.
Mary had no little.
Ditto pork steak in a New Orleans

Louis Gallo

Mexican restaurant.
Gather all the male brutes into a corral
and toss raw, bloody meat into it—
watch them kill each other for the
juiciest loin. Until they go extinct.
Ok with me . . . problem is,
flowers taste terrible. I know, I once
ate a magnolia leaf. We'll change
that. Deacidify. Imagine sweet olive
(oh what a sublime smell!) that tastes good—
a new restaurant in town: Botanical Gardens.
Who's hungry? And there's always hibiscus
which makes one tasty tea even as it
lowers your blood pressure!
Viva flowers!

Old Age

Something you can't name
fiddles with your mind
the way you roll a cat's eye
between fingers to warm it up.
Things happen before they happen–
you can't keep pace;
years lope along
like stripes on a highway.
At long last
butterflies flutter in the yard,
tiny women they are,
and the sun drips honey
into niches.
But too late–you aren't you
anymore.
You drop a tiny seed
into the moist black hole
scooped out with your own hands.
The screeches besiege you:
not now, yes now, not now,
slapping your face silly
like those molten girls
long ago, indignant
you could possibly
want so much.

Old Library at Lee Circle

for my sister

My father wept when they tore down
the stately old library at St. Charles
and Lee Circle. Even the general,
a brass memory patinaed green,
frowned from high on his Ionic pedestal
coated with pigeon droppings.

We raced up the heady flight of stairs,
though Dad, young still, took them slowly.
It was mandatory to wrap our arms
around the smooth, cool columns at the top,
for they seemed to proclaim
a rite of passage.

We followed him into a massive room
dense with musty old wood and leather
and up narrow metal stairwells to the stacks.
It was an expedition to reach those books
lining the shelves like somber emotions,
entombing wisdom we kids feared.

When Dad found his niche, he would whisper,
"Now you go play while I look around."
And scamper we did, up and down the aisles,
trying to suppress whelps and giggles

WHY IS THERE SOMETHING RATHER THAN NOTHING?

that seemed profane in silence
so intense it pummeled our ears.

We couldn't wait to find one of the glass tiles
separating each floor from the other.
The thick, smooth glass felt like stone,
polished quartz, opal. It was so opaque
we could see only vague, dim splotches
on the other side—ancient creatures swaying
near the bottom of some forgotten sea.
We curled up on that glass because
it was embedded near the lights,
and warm, in an otherwise
chilly and dim sanctuary.

In the end Dad wore us out.
He could stand forever glued to his spot
blowing dust from one book after another.
We'd nag, moan how tired we were, beg to go.
How could we have known that the library
was fated to be leveled, that in its place
would rise an angular steel high rise?
Or that Dad himself would be leveled?

Should we have begged him to stay
a moment longer? Stroked the glass
until a little rubbed off onto our skin?
The books failed to tell us that their pages,
like thick aqua glass, could never explain
the dark forms floating on the other side.

Louis Gallo

Ruth, you were too young to remember.
I was barely old enough myself.
I've scribbled this page for no good reason
beyond the urge to bury a worthless truth,
and perhaps thicken the glass a bit
so that if, again, we dare or need to peer
we will confront nothing more
than our own unfamiliar reflections.

Laundry

Sorting through socks, drawers and pajamas
I stare out the window at the orange moon,
a persimmon just above the pines.
It's not at all bad in this little washroom,
remote from the rest of the house, cozy,
humid, bright. Mounds of dirty clothes
and towels and sheets await my attendance.
I inhale their people odors with gratitude:
Cathy's almond lotion, the baby's strawberry
smears, five-year-old Claire's play dough.
I would stop to pray but there's no time.
Everyone needs fresh laundry by Monday
morning, tomorrow, so we can all begin again.
I pour Surf and powdered bleach
into the gurgling machine, a white load.
The scent of detergent twitches my nostrils
so I stick my head out of the window
and bite a chunk off the moon.
My mouth collapses as if I had licked alum.
Grandma always used to say, *Don't eat persimmons
until the first frost or you'll be surprised.*
But I'm too caught up in the task to whine.
The voices of my children float in
from the living room like tiny pink feathers.
Faintly I hear the commercial for Colgate Total
and feel reassured. The dog next door snarls.

Louis Gallo

Perhaps I have taken my duty too lightly.
I finish the piles at hand—
we're way past midnight now;
everyone in the neighborhood is asleep—
and I prowl the house like a thief for whatever
gloomy, tarnished items we have neglected.
Into the washer they go. Framed prints,
photo albums, cans of tuna stuck way back
in the cupboard, books, crusty hammers and
that lonely maul, dusty unopened packages
of forty-watt light bulbs, my old Winchester,
Cathy's sewing machine, her bicycle, Claire's Legos,
Maddie's doll house . . . I'm sweating with joy now,
this is the way to run a family . . .
my Hopi tom-tom, IRS records, armchairs,
the sofa and microwave, even the bathtub,
getting the ablution of their lives, yes, yes,
cleansed, bleached, starched, sparkling.
I pull the moon in from its black swatch of sky,
no longer a persimmon but a tiny forlorn grape,
toss it in with the rest. At this rate I might
salvage the entire universe before dawn
though as Grandma used to say, *It's always
what you don't count on that happens.*
Sure enough, I'm too tired and frayed
to go on. There's just so much to do,
so little soap left, no static sheets at all
or spot remover, Goop for the tougher blotches.
So I wash my hands of this eternal mission

WHY IS THERE SOMETHING RATHER THAN NOTHING?

and dive into the machine myself,
headfirst, fully clothed, filthier than you
can imagine.

I spin and spin with the suds, bounce off
the stuff I've dumped in, feel myself
sucked into an ever-tightening vortex
at the center. Grandma said as much:
You never realize you've gone too far until *you have.*
I expect to meet her in here any time
along with all the dead uncles and ancestors splendid
enough to take your breath away–Sargon I, Abraham,
Pericles, Hadrian, Charles the Bald, every other
notorious Charles, Joan of Arc, Rasputin. . .
But the cycles are so thorough
we're reduced to elementary particles now
just as the sun threads its web across the horizon.
Nothing so pristine as a proton.
I gasp with pleasure at the sight–
everything reduced to invisible spheres of pure beauty,
even us, Cathy and the kids, myself,
patterns of glitter, cleaner than delight,
this home of homes, where no one ever dreams
they're away or in need.

Laocoön & Sons—Moving and Storage

I pissed off the gods
because I warned that their Trojan horse
was a trap—I a Trojan priest,
I pissed off the gods in general
for making love to a woman
in plain sight of sacred images.
They sent vipers, tubes of horror,
to crush me and my sons
and some say I survived,
not out of divine mercy
but to suffer grief forever.

WHY IS THERE SOMETHING RATHER THAN NOTHING?

Well, what the stupid gods missed
was that I squeezed the serpents
to death with my bare hands
and we escaped to America
where we get by with the family business.

Hauling, storage, hauling storage,
day in, day out . . .
sometimes I wish I had never
killed those snakes,
accepted the fate of my boys and me,
died in a kind of strange glory.
This American dream festers
in all of us, hauling, storage,
day in, day out . . .
one step ahead of creditors today,
one behind tomorrow.
Back home I was adulated,
Esteemed a tragic hero;
here I amount to a meager statistic
longing for retirement and a woeful
monthly check from social security.
My sweet, dutiful boys have succumbed
to street crack, cheap tricks and rage.
O Columbia the gem of the ocean
shed your artificial tears for me.

Distance Equals Rate X Time

No doubt it's as futile hating an abstraction
as rolling that boulder up the hill eternally.
But I do anyway. I hate time. I have always
hated it. And I don't mean the tick-tock
of your snooze clock. Why is it one o'clock?
Who decreed it? I say it's ten billion o'clock
as the universe diasporas (away).

Quick, press the snooze! Opt out into the dream
where time ambushes itself. And look!
an old man up on the ledge screaming,
"Look what it did to me!" as he steps off
and floats down gently as a feather.
Ashes not to ashes but nothing at all.
I did not sign this contact.

And those damned physicists,
surely the smartest people in the world,
tell us that at the sub-atomic level
there is no time. Where's the nearest
electron microscope I can dive into?
Sure, small and cramped, but forever!

I'll take rate, I'll take distance . . .
make that time equals distance divided
by rate—and I'm at a standstill,

WHY IS THERE SOMETHING RATHER THAN NOTHING?

which equals zero.
Whoa, cry the mathematicians,
you can't divide anything by zero;
it has no value. I'm doing it anyway!

Time is not a bone you can clench
between your teeth. It smells, though,
when somebody dies. That gorgeous word
deliquescence. Write your Mama soon,
friend, the caboose approaches.

Listening to Scarlatti While Awaiting My Daughter
to Cross the Drill Field

I like the harpsichord's twang and pizzicatos.
Reminds me of Wallace Stevens
on whom my child is being tested
right now in a stone building across
the field. I have come to fetch her home
as tiny snowflakes sweep into the
half-cracked window of my old, dented van.
I picked up some mocha stout and a few
pouches of curried lentils with saffron
rice at Kroger on the way. I like curry, I like
Wallace Stevens:

you do not play things as they are/
when you play them on the glue guitar

I love my daughter. Yesterday
the engine malfunction light flashed
upon my dash. I needed a new gas cap—
bought one at an auto supply store
for twenty bucks.
Had to plaster on a heating patch
to assuage my aching lower back.
I like wind—sometimes.
I like being here. And to think,
throughout most of history I wasn't.

WHY IS THERE SOMETHING RATHER THAN NOTHING?

Nor was my daughter. Nor Wallace
Stevens. Nor Scarlatti.
But the wind was, maybe snowflakes.

Maddie just called on her cellphone.
I see her trudging across the field
with a heavy backpack, her pea coat
and hair sashaying with the wind.
I like this moment, this privileged moment,
rarer than all of time, the past,
the present, this iotal speck,
a metaphysical snowflake.

A Special Case

Blink. Blink. Blink. I blink my eyes. Over and over, little windows. If I hold my head back, I see Lizard hanging from the ceiling. They put me on this porch. Blink. Hello, Lizard. I will catch you and watch your pink throat puff up like cotton candy. You aren't afraid of me. Red Bean is a member of the Legume family. Red Bean Legume. Sal Paretti. Marie Paretti. Johnny Young. Sandy Young. The cousins. I know their names. They live around the corner. They call me Pinhead. Mommy told Telephone I came out of the womb wrong. They clamped my head with pliers. Blink. Hello, Telephone. Who are you now? My aunt Rosalie. I can't go anywhere, not to the park or school or the lake. I don't walk right, Mommy says, and can't read or write. I can't learn anything like continents or streets or words. Pliers squeezed my brains. Sofia is the capitol of Bulgaria. I make horrible sounds that scare people. Animal sounds. Lizard doesn't say anything so I don't say anything. Lizard tells me secrets. So do Mosquito Hawk and Rat and Hummingbird. And Potato, Artichoke and Kumquat. Wood whispers to me. And Pewter Tankard from great grandmaw. Nails hold the house together. Air goes up, up, up. Moon comes down. Sometimes Moon is a fingernail. Rain is wet. I like rain music. Electricity is the flow of electrons from one pole to another. Electrons have negative charges. What is the capitol of Mars? Mom tells Telephone I'm hopeless. Dad drove away in a car named Studebaker and never came back. He went to

WHY IS THERE SOMETHING RATHER THAN NOTHING?

Baton Rouge, capitol of Louisiana. Because of me, Mom tells Telephone. I don't remember him except his smell, which lingers. Dr. Tichenor's Antiseptic. It burns your eyes. Noun is the name of a person, place or thing. I am a noun. Mom cries and cries and cries. Cry is a verb. She doesn't hear Lizard say hello. She doesn't see Moon. She sits in the dark room. When I blink too much, she tells me to stop, it looks ugly. Ugly is an adjective. I have a name but it's secret. Sal, Marie, Johnny and Sandy call me Pinhead. They don't know my name. If they did, they would say hello, Name. They're not bad like the ones who throw rocks and call me Vegetable. Rocks belong to the Mineral family. Rocks say they are sorry to hurt me. All I do is rock on the swing. Rock is a verb. When I go inside I sit on the sofa. The sofa is brown. I like Sofa. It tickles me. Then I sleep and dream about Swing. I dream I swing into the sky and meet Angels. Angels have no bodies. Angels tell me hello. I do not blink. Sal went to Kindergarten today. Poor Sal. Lucky Sal. I will never go to Kindergarten because I'm hopeless. Lizard teaches me, Moon teaches, Sofa teaches. Spider too. I thank them. I love them. I am not afraid of me. I am not afraid of anything. Distance equals rate times time. Sometimes I see Sal walking home from school right behind Judy France. Judy has the name of a country. The capitol of France is Paris. Sal pants after Paris. Judy is so pretty I kiss her in my dreams. And she kisses me back. Dream loves me. Dream makes me better. Kindergarten is a dream of light. Nothing can travel faster than the speed of light.

    Except me.

About the Author

Two volumes of Louis Gallo's poetry, *Crash* and *Clearing the Attic*, will be published by Adelaide in the near future. A third, *Archaeology*, has been published by Kelsay Books; Kelsay will also publish a fourth volume, *Scherzo Furiant*, in the near future, and a fifth volume, *Leeway and Advent*. A novella, "The Art Deco Lung," will be published in *Storylandia*. His work has appeared or will shortly appear in *Wide Awake in the Pelican State* (LSU anthology), *Southern Literary Review, Fiction Fix, Glimmer Train, Hollins Critic,, Rattle, Southern Quarterly, Litro, New Orleans Review, Xavier Review, Glass: A Journal of Poetry, Missouri Review, Mississippi Review, Texas Review, Baltimore Review, Pennsylvania Literary Journal, The Ledge, storySouth, Houston Literary Review, Tampa Review, Raving Dove, The Journal (Ohio), Greensboro Review,* and many others. Chapbooks include *The Truth Changes, The Abomination of Fascination, Status Updates* and *The Ten Most Important Questions*. He is the founding editor of the now defunct journals, *The Barataria Review* and *Books: A New Orleans Review*. His work has been nominated for the Pushcart Prize several times. He is the recipient of an NEA grant for fiction. He teaches at Radford University in Radford, Virginia.

www.ingramcontent.com/pod-product-compliance
Lightning Source LLC
Chambersburg PA
CBHW071418070526
44578CB00003B/601